About the Author

Steve spent much of his life as a CEO in the insurance space. After seeing that government was not all it was cracked up to be, Steve ran for President of the United States in 2016 with the intent to return common sense to public service. Steve created a Colorado 2018 ballot initiative which redirects fines to victims and charities instead of government coffers.

The Best of Intentions – 50 Thoughts on Freedom

Steve Kerbel

The Best of Intentions – 50 Thoughts on Freedom

Olympia Publishers
London

www.olympiapublishers.com
OLYMPIA PAPERBACK EDITION

A CIP catalogue record for this title is
available from the British Library.

ISBN: 978-1-80074-772-2

First Published in 2022

Olympia Publishers
Tallis House
2 Tallis Street
London
EC4Y 0AB

Printed in Great Britain

Dedication

For Socorro, Matthew and Melissa. You are the wind beneath my wings, and my work to make this world better is for you and all of my precious family members here now and still to come.

Acknowledgements

Having spent most of my life with a comfortable, yet highly inaccurate perspective with regard to the way power over others is used and abused, this book is a result of many eye-opening experiences. While expressing gratitude for people who abuse their power in their own self-interests may seem strange, had it not been for these people I would never have opened my eyes to reality. Mostly, I thank the people who have fought battles big and small, in the interests of holding back a tidal wave of powerful special interests who would prefer to take advantage of myriad common people in order to feather their nests and feed their addictions to power over the innocent. I have learned volumes from them all, and this has placed me in the position to write this book. I hope that the readers will accept my perspective and band together to hold off this tidal wave for generations to come. I wish you all the best, and you have my eternal gratitude.

Part 1 – The Best of Intentions.

Preface:

There is an ongoing struggle between two basic schools of thought. On one hand, there are those who are more concerned about society as a whole, and on the other, there are some who are more concerned about leaving the individual to manage their lives based on their own decisions. Many inconsistencies exist, as neither viewpoint is pure in their positions, but if these gray areas are left out of the discussion for now, these are the foundations of political thought in the United States.

The existence of government and its self-proclaimed power over the people is an anomaly. Both foundational groups fight over control of government, and as the pendulum swings back and forth from one group to the other, those in power use that control to further what they believe are their causes. There is one commonality, however. Those who prefer less government interference use their periods of control to benefit their interests. Those who prefer more government interference use their periods of control to benefit their interests as well.

Government is a tool. It can make some people wealthy beyond belief while making others poor. It can elevate some people to unimaginable heights. It can destroy lives of others. It can permit some people to live and force others to die. Most people do not consider the absolute power of government and the destruction it willfully, and seemingly carelessly, perpetrates every hour of every day of every year.

Without realizing it, this is the real reason why people fight over control of government with such intensity, hostility, vigor and vitriol. Most people have these basic foundations... preferring societal protections versus individual freedoms. Those who achieve the realization of the sheer power of government and the lack of care, concern and compassion that governments possess are very rare. After all, it is government which controls the education system for the most part, and it would be contrary to the goals of government to instill this foundation into young minds.

It is a given that both schools of thought will use their periods of control of government to benefit their interests. A group which benefits from war and incarceration will create more international conflict and legislate more prohibitions and stiffer penalties for basically victimless crimes. A group which benefits from one form of energy production over another will legislate advantages for one type of energy producers, and disadvantages for other energy producers.

These two foundational groups have biases. One bias is in favor of successful people to enjoy their successes and respect the sacrifices that they made to achieve them. The other bias is against successful people's ability to reap the rewards from their sacrifices and to distribute those rewards among the society as a whole. The bias against successful people will paint these people as selfish villains who take advantage of those who struggle to survive. The bias in favor of successful people will argue that fewer people will take the risk to innovate if there is no financial benefit for taking the risk.

Both foundations have real beliefs and altruistic beginnings. But what is lacking in the view from those who are willing to give up freedom for the perception of security is the two-headed monster that they feed in attempting this. If people cannot be trusted, placing more people, who also cannot be trusted, with an excess of power over other people is a formula for disaster. Having the magic blessing of government instilled upon people, given the power of government, does not make them any different. No one will act properly all the time. Some people will act badly from time to time if it suits them. Some people will act badly all the time, no matter if they possess government credentials or not.

Chapter 1

Your Freedom Should End when it Negatively Impacts my Freedom

Rights are a funny thing. We all want them. We all think we have them. In reality, most people don't understand what is the difference between a right, an entitlement, and tyranny. In reality, actual rights are natural. Rights are not supposed to be bestowed by a government. What are natural rights? The right to live is the most basic natural right. According to Thomas Jefferson, the natural rights include the right to life, liberty, and the pursuit of happiness. His vision of the fledgling United States government is that it should never encroach on these natural rights.

Jefferson recognized that governments throughout modern history did little other than encroach on the natural rights of the people. So, the United States was designed for self-rule by leaving the people in control of government instead of the other way around. It was a brilliant design, however with the growth of government that occurred in the following centuries, the amount of individual freedom that we have in the United States today is infinitely less than the subjects of King George III maintained in the pre-revolutionary times.

There is always a good reason for doing a bad thing. Talented politicians are gifted with the skill of making bad things look like good things in order to get what they want. Any scholar who studies the history of various prohibitions in United States history should be keenly aware of the fact that these prohibitions were rooted more in selfish interests than the good of the society. Students of recent international conflicts would likely discover that the impetus for these conflicts usually had a self-serving benefit, while the public was rallied into supporting the conflicts as a result of clever misinformation and spin. When government picks winners and losers in private enterprise, and these selections benefit the politicians who legislate this result, the public is informed that the legislation of winners and losers supports the greater good.

In most cases, the citizens who support these bad actions do so with the best of intentions. They have placed their trust in representatives who have convinced them that they would represent the people in good faith. It is the government officials who take advantage of this higher power to feather their own nests and enhance their own careers. There is a certain pride that the citizens have that makes them look the other way when the people they support become bad actors. It is not uncommon for people to become apologists for the bad actions of politicians that they supported. One must only look at the history of presidential impeachments and the strict party line support or opposition to recognize that party affiliation is paramount to right and wrong in nearly every situation.

Considering the fact that government is not a credible decider of the boundaries of freedom, where should the lines be drawn? Where is that magic line where someone else's freedom has gone too far, and their actions have negatively affected you? If you are damaged by someone else exercising their freedoms, in what way are you damaged? If you have lost your life or lost your property as a result of another, that is easy to pinpoint. If you are injured or maimed as a result of the actions of another, that is also simple to identify.

In today's world of easily-offended people, some people claim that the words of other people so negatively impacted them that they suffered damages. Some people clamor for the freedom of speech as called for in the First Amendment to the Constitution to be limited. They are willing to give up the most basic of freedoms in order to make them feel safer. This is the slipperiest of slopes to a people who pride themselves in their freedoms. Previous generations were taught that 'sticks and stones may break my bones, but words will never hurt me'. Certainly, words can be hurtful, but it is a crucial component of survival to be able to ignore hurtful words. Granting government the ability to control speech would be the last nail in the coffin of a nation envisioned by its founders.

It is important to realize that every law carries penalties, and enforcers will be hired to enforce the laws. Enforcement has no bounds, up to and including causing the death of the suspected violator during pursuit or incarceration. Is it even imaginable to picture a society where all speech is monitored, and people who utter illegal words or phrases are subject to arrest and prosecution? Such a country did exist. It was a nightmare called the Union of Soviet Socialist Republics, better known as the USSR. If cooler heads do not prevail, and government is granted the power to control speech, the USA moves one step closer to becoming the USSR. It is scary that some people in the USA actually have become apologists for the founders of the USSR, but this will be addressed in future chapters.

A basis for the argument of where freedoms go too far and cause injury to others creates massive room for interpretation. If one person exercises their freedom and presents themselves in a way so as to cause other people to be uncomfortable, should that person's freedom to present themselves in this way be restricted? If a person's actions in public make other people feel at risk as a result of those actions, although no one is harmed, should those actions be restricted? Should penalties only apply if an injury actually occurs rather than if others perceive that they could potentially be at risk from those behaviors? And what is truly an injury? If one group feels that the in private actions of others violates their vision of morality, should those private actions be banned? If there is conflicting information with regard to the damages caused by some actions, should the society at large be forced to comply with new laws which recognize one viewpoint over another, by assigning credibility to one person over another?

The history of American legislation is riddled with examples of new laws which appeared as a result of one bad apple spoiling the barrel. More laws and regulations exist in the United States than any group of attorneys or politicians can identify. Nearly every product or service in the United States is either illegal or regulated. There are myriad arms of government which investigate, enforce and punish people who either intentionally or unintentionally violate any laws or regulations. These enforcers benefit with pay raises and promotions for prosecuting violators, no matter how negligible the alleged violations may have been. Clearly the existence of this type of enforcement is the antithesis of freedom. Clearly government will never punish itself for the creation of these laws and regulations or the enforcement of them, even if it was later uncovered that the basis for these laws and regulations was self-serving rather than for the benefit of the public.

It is common for the public to formulate opinions based upon information provided from sources whom they deem to be credible. No matter what those sources may say, there are many people who will argue in favor of positions of which they have no personal knowledge, because they believe what other people have told them. This leads up to more prohibitive orders and legislation which angers opponents who believe the position of opposing sources of information, whom they deem to be the most credible.

This is where the argument of 'where does the freedom of one person negatively impact the rights of another person' really comes down to the grayest of areas. If a person ingests a substance in their living room while watching a movie, and goes to sleep, did that person harm you? If that same person causes harm to others in their care via physical harm or neglect, should that harm or neglect be illegal, or should everyone who engages in that behavior be subject to punishment regardless of the results of their actions. If a person possesses a firearm for defensive purposes and never uses it should the mere possession of that firearm be illegal? Or should there only be penalties for actions such as causing injury or death to other people while using the firearm or improper management of the firearm which resulted in the accidental injury or death to others?

Pre-emptive legislation such as actions which do not cause harm to others creates a huge debate when the discussion of individual freedom arises. The resulting increase in government enforcement of these victimless activities results in today's reality that the majority of people who are currently imprisoned did not hurt anyone else. This is another example of where the line should be drawn with regard to individual freedom versus the perception of security. In the end, people are going to do what they are going to do. If the only actions which are illegal are actions which create victims of innocent people, that is closer to the vision of natural rights as identified by Thomas Jefferson.

Will prohibition style laws against victimless actions protect innocent people? It's hard to say. It's even harder to interpret the damages to other people that result from the free actions of others. A current case in point is the Covid-19 pandemic. No one can really agree on where the lines should be drawn. No one can really agree as to which preventions are most effective. There are those who are terrified and are fine with severe restrictions on the actions of other people. There are others who prefer to make their own choices. There are still others who believe that reckless choices of others can cause illness or death to innocent people. There are also others who think that the entire situation is fake. Still others who created vaccines to prevent most people from becoming infected. Others who don't accept that the vaccine is safe or effective. Others who want to stop other people from entering areas who have not received the vaccine. Others who believe strongly in wearing masks. Others who don't believe that masks are effective and see them as a symptom of subservience. And who can really tell who damaged who... The pandemic revealed the worst-case scenario in trying to determine where someone else's freedom ends because they harmed another.

These types of arguments will go on for as long as the discussion of a nation which is subject to a government of the people, by the people and for the people, and individual freedom remains as a foundation for the United States. The line is not simply drawn. When the desire for individual freedom is ultimately ridiculed by those who place the perception of security over personal liberty, and that ridicule is adopted by the majority, the entirety of the goals of maintaining a free country are forever lost.

Many people tend to gloss over one important, material fact. Pure democracy is simply mob rule tyranny. That is why we are a constitutional republic, not a democracy. Constitutional is the key. For example, in a pure democracy, 50% +1 voters could throw 50% -1 voters in prison for saying hello, absent a constitution which expressly forbids laws which restrict freedom of speech. The constitution limits the power of government by stating which individual freedoms must never be taken away by any actions of government, including lawmakers. The existence of a constitution and the required adherence to this constitution by lawmakers is what protects the minority from the tyranny of pure democracy. Elected representatives make laws after swearing to uphold the constitution in their duties, in order to preserve the limitations to government that are included in much of the constitution.

Now, many people continually try to get around these

constitutional limitations of government power due to their opinions and self-interests, and that is bad. Leaving the constitution, especially the bill of rights, unfettered is the only remaining tool to keep the country as designed as the ebbs and flows of public opinion pass through time. Some people refer to the country as a Democracy without really understanding what we really are and why this is the case. If one refers to democracy as a concept, as in we get to vote for people and other issues, that is correct and must be left unobstructed. That is the democracy that gets threatened if our votes are not allowed or accurately counted but to call the country a Democracy is grossly incorrect and actually becoming a pure Democracy must never be allowed to happen. Without a constitution as our backbone, we are not what we say we are... a free country. The Far Left cannot achieve what they want to achieve, so long as the Constitution remains the law of the land. This is why we hear Leftist politicians refer to our Republic as a Democracy. It is only through pure Democracy that a one-party dictatorship becomes possible.

Chapter 2

It Will be Different this Time, and the Definition of Insanity.

People are people, and power is a drug. When people are granted too much power over other people, it is inevitable that this power will be abused. One main reason why strong, central governments fail is this very reason. Local governments are nowhere near innocent of the abuse of power, but these abuses are easier to correct. When a person has power over one hundred people, those one hundred people are closer to the situation and have the ability to remove the abuser from office. In a strong central government, it is not unusual for a person to have power over one hundred million people instead. While it is possible that the abuser of power over those one hundred million people can be removed by them, it is more typical that fifty million people support the bad actor, and fifty million people oppose the bad actor. They spend all their time fighting each other instead of removing the bad actor.

Left alone with power over one hundred million people, the bad actor will create legislation which strengthens their power, making it impossible to remove them or their cronies. This is what has happened throughout human history when a strong, central government is allowed to exist. It always solidifies its power and creates a massive infrastructure which punishes detractors.

So, while many perceive that a more central, socialist government would benefit those in need, the result is always the same... a punitive, dictatorial, aggressive person will take the reins and kill its own people by the millions. The same argument is happening today. The cost of living has become unmanageable for millions of people. In desperation, they clamor for a large, central government to provide social benefits for the masses. While leftist extremists utter the exact same words as Vladimir Lenin published in 1897 (speaking of the evils of capitalism), they also proclaim that the same thing cannot happen here. They have become apologists for modern politicians who want to restrict freedoms and build a strong central government, because that is the only way they can envision a solution to their problems.

The definition of insanity, according to many, is as follows: The definition of insanity is to do the same thing over and over again and expect different results.

One can assume that if fewer people are placed in control of the masses, those people will make decisions for the masses. With fewer people in a decision-making capability, the masses will have less representation. If the masses have little or no representation, no power at all in decisions which affect them, not only is personal freedom and all the benefits which go along with it lost forever, any action of the individual which does not benefit those in control becomes illegal and grounds for punishment.

If the insanity of growing a strong, central government is allowed to continue, this great experiment ends in abject failure. Anyone who dares to disagree with proponents of a large federal government is called 'selfish' by those people. Arguments that these types of moves would result in a

Soviet-style situation here in the USA are met with violence in some universities. There are those who believe that they have a right to your possessions and your services. They believe that rights are not freedoms, instead rights are claims to your actions and your assets. These same people place society at such a high level that they don't mind if innocent people are harmed as a result of their endeavors. The view that 'you've got to break some eggs to make an omelet' is pervasive in the socialist or communist communities.

The desire for personal comforts at the expense of others is strong. People are quick to blame others for their lot in life. They blame the successful for their lack of success. They blame the wealthy for the existence of the poor. The only vehicle that they can muster which has the ability to take from you and give to them is government, and lots of it. To many, these concerns are legitimate. Life is hard and getting harder. Sadly, though, they seek to grow the very institution which is responsible for the increasing difficulty in the cost of living.

The bottom line is that it would indeed be different this time. The tyranny would be even worse as a result of more efficient surveillance of the masses by the few in power. The infrastructure of punishment would be even more invasive. The media would be even more tightly controlled and used to indoctrinate the masses to support the desires of the few in power. The schools would be even more stringent in only disseminating information which benefits the powerful. It would be easier to identify those who dare to speak against the state… and the indoctrinated masses would have to support the mass killings of the detractors or be punished themselves.

Chapter 3

Venezuela

Venezuela is a modern example of what happens in the end when proponents for a strong central government prevail. It's pretty much the same story as always. The wealthy are villainized, and government is directed to take their assets and spread them to everyone else. In self-defense, the wealthy take over the government and gain power as well. The people want more social services and give the power to a few people who inevitably abuse it. The country turns into a prison state with a few super wealthy and powerful people, and everyone else becomes a victim of it.

Venezuela today is very poor. The people have little to no food at times. The average man is losing twenty-four pounds per year. The Guaire river in Caracas is now nothing but raw sewage. Doctors are performing surgery by flashlight from time to time. People are escaping Venezuela by the millions. 'Collectivos' are the modern KGB there. Watching people, following people, killing people with abandon, destroying property, burning buildings, etc. A government licensed mafia to watch over the people and force their subservience, the Collectivos, are an example of what happens in every strong, central government turned to a dictatorship.

It was not always this way. In 1970, Venezuela was the

wealthiest country in Latin America. The quality of life was very good. The Venezuelan economy was able to compete with other major economies around the world. In 1976, the oil industry was seized and nationalized. The revenues from the nationalization of the oil industry were spent providing government services. On the surface, that doesn't sound too bad. But as the level of government services increased, more and more people became dependent on government for their survival. As the government seized assets from the wealthy to redistribute to everyone else, the people cheered.

As the national income fluctuated, rather than make changes to these benefits, government incurred debt. It started printing money rather than balancing its budget. The inevitable result of deficit spending and printing money is inflation, and the people were able to buy fewer and fewer products and services for the same amount of money as inflation spiraled out of control. The population was no longer able to figure out how to survive without government support.

Enter Hugo Chavez in the 1990s. Chavez replaced the former two-party system with a one-party system. He continued to spend far in excess of the revenues. He grew the state more and more. He gave money to other countries, growing the debt even further. Following the public reliance on the state was an overwhelming public fear. Fear of speaking out. Fear of survival. What was once a prosperous country was destroyed in a matter of decades by a move toward Socialist policies and a strong central government which never had enough control to satisfy its leader.

For a while, the people had what they wanted. In the end, the price they paid for this government reliance was far more destructive than any benefit they received. It was common for Venezuelans to scoff at Cuba and say that what happened in Cuba could never happen in Venezuela. At the completion of this cycle, it ended up being even worse in Venezuela than it was in Cuba even with the best of intentions.

There are many examples of the results of people becoming too dependent on government which always evolves into an instrument of tyranny. It has happened over and over again. But it always starts the same way. People hate the wealthy and use government to deprive the wealthy of their wealth and spread it out to the rest of society. Government gets drunk on power and the people are gravely harmed.

To see so many people fighting so hard for the same system in the USA shows that our education system has selectively failed to educate them in the realities of history. After all, government controls the curriculum. Government has an un-ending desire to grow itself. If government had adequately taught students that government was fallible and too much government can be inherently destructive, it might be shooting itself in the foot.

Venezuela should be seen as a modern example of the pitfalls of a strong central government and the creation of public dependence on government for survival. Sadly, this example, as well as all the others, is largely ignored.

Chapter 4

Changing Laws to Keep Only One Party in Power.

A move toward one party rule should set off deafening alarm bells to anyone with a grasp of history. One party rule is always a component of a country leading towards dictatorship. A government controlled by the people requires constant conflict. It requires constant give and take. Without multiple inputs from various viewpoints, it becomes like a football game where there is one offense who is always on the field, with no defense to provide resistance. Without resistance, one team runs the field, over and over again. Human nature will always go too far without such resistance. This concept goes hand in hand with the reality that power is a drug, and the desire for power is a weakness at best, and a disease at worst. A one-party system must be resisted with all the might of all the people, or dictatorship is sure to follow.

It should be apparent to all that as the Democrats currently have a slight majority in the leadership of the federal government, they are doing all they can to retain their power into perpetuity. Changing election laws to favor central control, ending the electoral college in favor of the most populous states overshadowing the will of the people in fly-over states, control of print media, broadcast media and social media, restriction of third-party competition in debates and ballot access, and identifying local election laws, which would require a voter to identify themselves on par with slavery and segregation laws, are all hot items at this point. In order to control the people, the citizenry must be disarmed, and this is a major goal of the Left. In order to achieve complete political dominance, the Bill of Rights must be significantly circumvented. It is the first ten amendments to the Constitution which were designed to limit the power of government and allow the people to stay in control of the government. Certainly, the first and second amendments are the most crucial in this regard. If the people can legally speak their minds, worship as they see fit, report the events of the day to the people, get together to peacefully meet for any reason, and redress the government when they decide there is a legitimate reason to do so, it is pretty hard for a totalitarian government to steal away the basics of freedom from the people. It is also a consistent action of a government which intends to seize control and rule the people instead of the other way around, to take away the citizens' ability to defend themselves.

Pre-emptive prohibition laws such as the attempt to disarm a peaceful citizenry is an example of the Left's attempt to render the Second Amendment basically meaningless. Also, attempts at the legislation of free speech is a stab in the heart of the First Amendment. Fear is the weapon of choice. People are willingly open to giving up more and more of their freedoms in exchange for the perception of government protection. The more that the Left can build up the fear of firearms in the general public, the likelihood increases that more and more gun laws will pass with the support of the majority of the public.

There is not only a pendulum of control between the political parties; there is also a pendulum of public opinion. Over the last two hundred plus years, there have been plenty of movements supported by the people which would take away personal freedoms. Plenty have attempted to render the Bill of Rights powerless, one by one. The consistency to keep the Bill of Rights in place as the backbone of the land falls in the hands of the Supreme Court. This is another reason why the partisans want to take control of the Supreme Court. In reality, the Supreme Court must never become a partisan institution. The only responsibility of the Supreme Court is to interpret disputes in such a way as to keep the Constitution as the overriding law of the land. The Left has floated the idea of adding Supreme Court Justices that will further their need to circumvent the constitution in order to take the power from the people and give it to themselves. While partisanship should never enter any deliberation of a constitutional matter, the Left is hell bent to change the Supreme Court into a partisan institution in order to serve their agenda.

If the supporters of the 'D' team thought more deeply as to the long-term results of their actions rather than rooting for their team to win over the other team, it would be inconvenient to those who press for totalitarian control. It is this tribalism that clouds the reasonable thinking of our society. From the outside looking in, one would notice that it is extremely common for a supporter of one side to agree with everything their team does. But when someone from the other team does the exact same thing, it is horrible and evil. As long as this tribalism is as pervasive as it is, it allows those in power to continue to further their agendas rather than being fully accountable to the people who elected them.

Many people are aware of gerrymandering. Gerrymandering is done by both parties, and is used to make it easier for them to win future elections by defining certain districts in a way that is beneficial to them. Looking at what is happening today makes gerrymandering look like innocent child's play. If the founding fathers were alive today, they would most certainly be labeled as enemies of the state for speaking the same words that they did in the formation of the USA. Had we heeded their warnings, we would not be facing such a tragedy as being promoted with great intensity by the far left.

With respect to the Electoral College, one should notice that the only supporters of the National Popular Vote Compact are Democrats. The National Popular Vote Compact is a movement in which states, who assign their electoral votes to one candidate, agree to transfer their electoral votes to whichever candidate wins the national majority in a presidential election. Essentially, the states who join this compact have agreed that the will of their voters is less important than the will of the voters in other states. They have given up their right to vote in favor of party interests. It's no secret that the larger-population states such as California and New York vote overwhelmingly Democrat, and those totals pad the national count in their favor. So, states like Colorado have agreed to ignore the decision of Coloradans if California and the other larger states disagree. It's a travesty for sure. But while the

Supreme Court would surely block this deed before it actually resulted in any real impact, it would still be amusing to see the reactions of Democrats in the future should the Republicans win the national popular vote in the future.

What seems most disillusioning is that these attempts to control future elections are glaringly transparent. But as transparent as they may be, the Leftist supporters blindly cheer on the team without regard to the future results of their actions... kind of like the move to socialism in Venezuela.

Chapter 5

Do the Powerful Really Care about What's Best for their Subjects?

Let's take a deep dive into the psyches of those who crave power. Sure, they may make statements which indicate that they have care, concern and compassion for those they rule, but in the end, what matters most to them is keeping and increasing their power.

Even Abraham Lincoln was quoted as saying that, given the choice, he would not abolish slavery if the Union was to be broken down, and his top priority was maintaining the Union. He hated slavery, but his Emancipation Proclamation was a military measure to demoralize and destabilize the rebellious South. It covered states he did not govern but did not apply in slave holding states that remained under his jurisdiction.

Those in power will reluctantly throw their subjects a bone strictly for the purpose of maintaining that power. Many people in power would be identified as sociopaths. What is a sociopath? Basically, a sociopath lacks a conscience. This is why we see so many politicians saying one thing and doing the exact opposite. They are highly concerned with 'optics'. How the people perceive what they are doing is what matters. The powerful use that power to make their own lives better. The realities of their subjects are only important when the topic of their removal from power surfaces.

The truth is simple. Powerful people care about their subjects when it is convenient for them or does not get in the way of their personal desires. It is quite common for people to place their trust in other people to make decisions on their behalf, but it is rare for those decisions to be consistently forthright for the benefit of their subjects.

As the breadth of power grows, a person craves more and more. They start to covet that power as something they cannot live without. This is why we must resist central control in the United States. Local governments can be controlled by local people. National governments are beyond the control of the people. Theoretically, the people can still control a national government, but the reality of the situation is vastly different.

Looking at the realities of mainstream media, it is not difficult to identify that mass media publishes what those in power want it to publish. Those who control media also have a significant stake in controlling government, and vice versa. Outsiders such as third parties are all but eliminated from the public eye by mass media. It is inconvenient to the goals of the powerful to allow alternative viewpoints which may dovetail better with the sensibilities of the majority of voters to be presented to these voters by mainstream media. It is better for those in power to only present alternative viewpoints in a way as to ridicule them. It is most common for mainstream media to present third parties when someone within those parties says or does something which discredits their movements, rather than when someone says or does something that the majority would appreciate.

If popular media was to present balanced and accurate information, it would be easier for alternative views and movements to gain traction among the majority of voters. Remember that what matters most to the powerful is the maintenance and growth of that power. With the control that the powerful have over mass media in print, broadcast and social media, that control will be utilized heavily for the purpose of excluding viable competition from public acceptance.

Historically, news publications were mostly news, and included a small and easily identifiable opinion or editorial section. The evolution of twenty-four-hour news sources have completely flipped this relationship. A visit to many websites of twenty-four-hour news providers would expose the fact that most of what is presented as news is actually opinion or editorial... and the political spin of that former news source is easily identifiable by the attacks on whoever the opposition to the management of that source may be. Unfortunately, the majority of viewers identify with one major group or the other, and feed on the attacks against their perceived opposition. This is why the viewership of these networks remains significant, and why the public furthers whatever argument they heard on their preferred network.

There is a scary trend, however. The vast majority of news organizations use their pulpits to further the cause of electing more Democrats. When the news media and the educational system are all slanted toward the Left, the people who listen to these sources also absorb the fear that they are supposed to absorb. Fear is the prime motivator of people to vote for Leftist candidates. As this trend continues to gain steam without resistance, the United States heads toward becoming a one-party system.

As previously stated, the real motivation for the powerful is to increase or maintain their power. Having one party control the media and the education system is a key component in achieving that goal. So, it seems clear that those in power might actually care about what is best for their subjects... but will place this as a lower priority than keeping in power.

Chapter 6

Taxation – More Money in Government Coffers Means Less Money in your Pocket.

The less money that you have, the less freedom that you have. It's that simple. People who support a grand scheme of central planning are only too happy to dictate your entire life. A structure of rules which control every moment of every day. Behind each dictate is a reason why that dictate benefits those in control. Some people might prefer being told what to do, but even those people have a limit. Government has no limit. It will never be satisfied with the amount of control it has over all the people... period.

While advocates for higher taxes (for everyone but them, that is) play the guilt card with abandon, they too don't see the big picture. They are all about redistributing wealth and care not to see what happens when this plan is allowed to evolve to fruition. Truthfully, what is done with current tax money? Lots of interest on the debt, lots of incarcerating people who never hurt anyone, lots of wars which should never have been fought, lots of money going to other countries, lots of money enforcing laws which were passed for self-serving reasons and lobbyists, lots of money on huge regulatory agencies that cause more damage to the people rather than being a helpful resource, and very little spent on what the people actually want.

How many times have you seen various jurisdictions vying for tax increases to fix roads which already had a budget to fix them, but that money was spent on something else? After those tax increases passed, were there attempts to direct it to other things, like new stadiums? Politicians know that people care about what matters to them. People want quality roads. But they pay for them over and over again and still never get them... right? The reason for this is because if they actually fixed the roads, people would stop agreeing to give them more money for fixing roads that never get fixed.

A person who does not support tax increases is not necessarily just selfish. More money in the hands of government is more money that is used to hurt innocent people. Less money in your pocket makes you more dependent on government. It's just that simple. Tyranny always follows dependence. To the powerful people, all that really matters is that the lowly populace complies with their edicts. Non-compliance is unacceptable and must be punished. In reality, the punished pays the punisher to punish them through taxation.

Chapter 7

The Social Contract

When a person objects to excessive rules, regulations and taxation, they are commonly met with an objection relating to a Social Contract. This is where the 'love it or leave it' argument will surface. You are told that you must agree to all these rules and try to change them if you can. If you don't agree, you can simply leave the city, state, country, etc… like it's that easy.

A social contract is not a new concept. It goes as far back as Plato. The funny thing is that whoever wants to force to you do something you don't want to do is only too happy to invoke the social contract. A social contract by definition, according to Oxford Languages, is 'an implicit agreement among the members of a society to cooperate for social benefits, for example by sacrificing some individual freedom for state protection. Theories of a social contract became popular in the sixteenth, seventeenth, and eighteenth centuries among theorists such as Thomas Hobbes, John Locke, and Jean-Jacques Rousseau, as a means of explaining the origin of government and the obligations of subjects.'

People from many viewpoints play the Social Contract card. But here's the rub… a contract requires consent. If you don't have the will or the resources to escape the onerous tyranny of your local social contract, does that mean that you consent to it? There are several types of recognized consent, such as implied, tacit or explicit. Explicit means that you agree to the terms without reservation. No social contract is explicit.

Lysander Spooner was an attorney in the 1800s, who argued in front of the Supreme Court against the social contract as a means of sanctioning government taxation. Spooner argued that a supposed social contract cannot be used to justify governmental actions such as taxation, because government will initiate force against anyone who does not wish to enter into such a contract. A legal and binding contract is entered into voluntarily and without coercion. Spooner also argued against slavery for the same reason. Today, it is the combination of accusing people of being greedy and selfish, combined with the social contract which is used by the left to berate those who disagree with the growth of government and its funding via forcible taxation.

The argument in favor of ever-increasing taxation is a key component in any plan which makes government larger, strips the individual of freedom and choices, and is another brick in a totalitarian wall. Had the United States not been created with individual freedom in mind, this would not matter. We are seemingly in a heavily orchestrated bait and switch scam that is being perpetrated by the left.

Chapter 8

Democratic Socialism

It's been said that under Democratic Socialism, government will still seize your business, but do it with a smile on their face. Over the years, there has been a serious taboo surrounding the term 'socialism' in the United States. Democratic Socialism appears to be a sort of a compromise. The problem is that proponents of democratic socialism fail to make the connection that any and all movements toward government control of personal needs makes the people become more reliant on that assistance.

A person who resorts to relying on government for their survival gets used to that situation. As a population becomes more and more dependent on government for their needs, the skills to fulfill these needs on their own gets rusty or non-existent. Throughout world history, countries which provided a high level of services to the population were only able to achieve this for a short period of time, and what followed was either a restructuring which stopped many benefits, or a complete failure of the country and an eventual collapse.

A more glaring and sinister result of moving in the direction of socialism is that government never voluntarily gives up its authority. Conversely, it always wants more. So, while providing something like health care would solve some problems and create still more, it is the progression that is the major concern. The more the people counted on the government for their support, the more the government would continue to legislate its own growth and its scope of power. With the current trajectory, it will not be too long before government begins to seize certain means of production, and that is the beginning of the end.

No matter the intent, there is always a danger to making a government too powerful and too involved in the lives of a people who are supposed to control it. The concept of controlling a government that provides your support is on the same plane as controlling the company with which you are employed. People just don't want to risk losing their means of support.

Many proponents of democratic socialism may not favor government seizing the means of production. Some actually do support this concept. When presented with historical evidence that this system never works, bankrupts countries, or spawns brutal dictatorships, the answer is always the same: 'it will be different here'. But history has proven again and again that all people who promoted socialism were proven wrong. It was not different anywhere.

It's a tough world we live in, and financial challenges can seem insurmountable. Many of us would prefer to have help with food, housing, health care and education. The thing is, there are better ways to solve these problems than giving more money to an institution which is only too happy to arrest you, destroy your businesses, destroy your livelihood and reputation, destroy innocent people here and abroad and build its base of power. Given the opportunity, all the flowers, clowns and rainbows which are attached to bombs will not end up killing fewer people.

Chapter 9

The End of an Experiment

The not-too-distant future will arrive before we know it. The result will be ugly. What is to follow has not happened yet, and many people will do all they can to avoid this scenario. The current mood of a slight majority of the people is likely to result in what you are about to experience in the next two chapters. It seems as if there is no stopping what is about to happen.

The future arrives...

It's over. They got what they thought they wanted. Everyone is the same, except for the few in power over the masses. Food is scarce. Poverty is rampant. Hope has disappeared from American life. The President of the United States has self-legislated the position into a new description. The Constitution is null and void. A dictator whose rule will never end and will be passed on to others of their choice or bloodline.

All self-defense tools have been confiscated. A government licensed mafia rules the streets, taking all they choose to steal, killing whoever they want with nothing to stop them. Inflation is in the thousands of percent. Government owns all means of production. Government grants jobs only to people who have complied with every edict throughout their lives. The others wander the streets until they too are killed at the hands of the government licensed mafia.

There is no need for education which teaches anything other than compliance with government desires. Education camps and rallies have replaced the universities which fought with all their might for a socialist, centrally-controlled government. Children are taken from their parents at an early age and are placed in various facilities which indoctrinate state values. There is no freedom of anything, let alone speech or religion. The press is under tight control of the government. The only information that people are allowed to consume must pass by government censors.

Religion is abolished. The state is the omnipotent force. Anyone who dares to practice any religion without state approval is severely punished. There is no means to redress grievances with the government. Anyone who dares to attempt this is convicted of treason and killed. No one can get together in groups for any reason, with the exception of when they are ordered by the state to gather for state reasons.

Lines are long for the basic necessities which must be acquired from government sources. If a person is instructed to perform any task, they have no right to decline regardless of their personal beliefs. The state is the alpha and the omega and exercises this power with relentless abandon. Everything that is done is monitored extensively, with layers of reporting the activities of each person. The dictator is quite paranoid and is convinced that every person is a threat to them. Killings of perceived enemies happen every day, and these killings are shown in all media, to discourage anyone from finding themselves on the wrong side of the dictator or the dictator's cronies.

The national anthem has been replaced with a song which glorifies the dictator, and it is mandatory for everyone to sing this song in public several times per day. 'Mandatory' is the word that is used more than any other by the dictator, closely followed by 'penalty'. The only real industry is war technology. There are constant parades which demonstrate the weaponry in the possession of the dictatorship. In order to look impressive to the rest of the world, state resources are heavily devoted toward athletics. Winning international athletic competitions is a matter of life and death.

Very few personal items which are desired by the people are permitted. There will be those who try to innovate replacements for many items, but it must be done in a clandestine fashion. The punishments for using unregulated items are severe. People are wandering the streets, searching for any scraps that can be used as food. Dysentery becomes the greatest killer in the land.

The air is filthy. The water is polluted. The streets in the outlying areas are covered with trash. Only the streets that are seen by the rest of the world are pristine. All access to internet is highly restricted. Power is sporadic at best. No unauthorized images of places in the US are allowed to be distributed outside the country. It is imperative to the dictator that the US is still represented as what it once was but no longer is. The USA has joined North Korea with the highest level of international ridicule in the world. The international community is well aware that these presentations of a great life in the USA are contrived. Many in the international community routinely attempt to expose the human rights violations in the USA, but those attempts are scoffed at by the dictator and their cronies.

Those still interested in politics and who have advocated for this strong, central government are no longer allowed to express their opinions. Even though they realize that the path that they fought for all their lives led to the current suffering, they cannot say this. But, if asked, many would still never agree that leaving people alone to live their lives without government interference can be beneficial to society as a whole.

In the end, due to immense poverty, lack of food and supplies with too many government restrictions on producing farmed foods, rampant disease, inflation, and overall tyranny, people will climb the border walls in order to escape. Eventually, the dictator will flee into hiding, and there will be an overall collapse of the United States.

What follows is a period of panic. Without every moment of the lives of the people centrally planned, and without every move being monitored and reported to the central government, the people do not know what to do. Survival is still at the forefront of the minds of the people. The formerly government-licensed mafia melts back into society and shares these realities with the people that they used to rule with iron fists.

Anarchy results. Not the anarchy which is described by some as a beautiful freedom with no government interference or disturbance of the peace. This situation results in new gangs trying to replace the collapsed government, each with the goal of stealing power for themselves. There are gangs of vigilantes as well, militias of sorts, which try to defend the weak from the actions of the gangs trying to steal power. These militias also tried to create themselves as the rulers of the people.

The desire for power being the sickness that it is, gangs of all types fight for the power to control other people. But the rules that these mafias create are inconsistent. What is acceptable behavior for them is not acceptable in the general public. Murder, rape, robbery, assault and kidnapping are fine if perpetrated by these mafias, but these same mafias would punish the public at large if they failed to follow the rules set down by these groups.

This situation ebbs and flows for a generation, until peaceful people started to assemble without the knowledge of these self-sanctioned leadership gangs.

Chapter 10

A Phoenix Rises from the Ashes...

Deep down, through all the damage and destruction caused by the dictator and subsequent gangs, the American spirit lies dormant. While it is impossible for anyone to try to innovate or to improve their own lives, this spirit lingers in the shadows, not to be seen. Some would say that this spirit was in our blood as Americans. Our culture has always been rebellious, and while that rebellious nature was quashed by totalitarian control, it is still in the genes of the people. It began to re-appear after the collapse of the totalitarian dictatorship and later events.

While many millions are murdered, others die as a result of the conditions, and hundreds of millions more were badly damaged during the previous administration, many of those who sat quietly by stand up and dust themselves off. They begin by growing food. They work to build a new infrastructure from the crumbling wreckage left behind. They work together to solve these immense problems that now could be solved without government interfering in all the solutions.

Society is mostly voluntary at this time. The people who can pitch in do pitch in. Slowly, the nation is rebuilt brick by brick... locality by locality. Being mindful of what they have been through, they work to avoid these previous mistakes in the future. As the Phoenix rises from the ashes and the nation reverts to a better time when the people were free, the American spirit kicks into high gear. After decades of decomposition, cities reappear. Former states re-organize, but are tightly controlled to stop them from getting out of control as they did in the past.

A generation passes. The new generation hears stories of what has previously happened. They are warned not to make the same mistakes. They do not for the most part, however they felt that there were good reasons to mandate some things. This begins the process anew. As the generations pass, there is always a good reason to build more government, force more compliance with that government, and rebuild an infrastructure of public benefits. The subsequent generations become reliant on those benefits, and press for a larger government with more public benefits. Taxes rise. Government infrastructure rise. Enforcement and incarceration rise. War flourishes.

...and the clamoring for socialism returns... and everyone who opposes it is just selfish.

Epilogue

So, You Think This Scenario is Impossible? It's Too Extreme? It Can't Happen Here?

To answer your question, let me suggest that you do your own independent research on the USSR, Venezuela, Cuba, China, North Korea, Israel, India, United Kingdom, Sweden, Norway, Poland, Czechoslovakia, Germany, Greece, Tanzania, Ethiopia, Guinea, Ethiopia, and many more. See how socialism worked for them. Some survived and moved away from the system. Others collapsed. Socialism always appeared for the same reasons. They hated the rich and wanted more for themselves, but their appetite for risk was outweighed by their hatred and desire to use government to level the playing field. It failed every time.

Part 2 –
50 Thoughts on Freedom

The following are a select collection of my daily observations which can be helpful in keeping us from being distracted by short term obsessions. For the health of our nation, which is intended to be free, these thoughts can be useful in remaining mindful of the bigger picture.

1) A proper constitution sets the parameters of the state. The amendments to the constitution must be the enemy of the state in order to achieve their initial goal. By its very nature, the state craves power. Limitless power. This is the nature of every government in human history. By limiting the power of the state, these amendments to the constitution are absolutely the enemy of the state. This is why the state always tries to get around the constitution. But the state is strong, and it is successful in making some people resent the constitution because it is inconvenient to the state. The more the state controls dissemination of information via schools and media, the less teeth remain in the Bill of Rights. Those people who listen to the state see the state as an omnipotent deity... exactly what the founders sought to prevent. In reality, an enemy of the state may be the best friend of the people... at least that is what Thomas Jefferson might say, if the state had not banned him in the names of San Francisco schools.

2) The mainstream media reports what they want to report, hides what they want to hide, and spins what they want to spin. The mainstream media creates polls which decide who is allowed in debates and who is excluded. The mainstream media has become more of an editorial source than an information source. The mainstream media is colluding to benefit one political party at the detriment of all the others. The mainstream media is influencing elections. The mainstream media is joining together and becoming closer and closer to state-run media, like Pravda. The first amendment guarantees freedom of the press. But what happens when the press does not do their jobs, bands together to silence or demonize opposition and competition, cancel historical events or figures, decide elections, and generally control the future of the nation? The schools now have competition. How would Thomas Jefferson have dealt with all of this? Oh, yeah… Thomas Jefferson is banned in San Francisco. This is a real problem.

3) It occurred to me that 'Let's Make a Deal' is pretty much like life itself. The show is basically a series of choices. People sit in the audience, waiting for their turn to make a choice. Some choices end up being good ones, some don't make much of a difference, and others are disastrous. One difference is that in real life, some choices we make are more educated and others are just pure luck. In life, most people make most choices hoping for the best result. Sometimes those choices end up really badly even though the choice seemed like the best one at the time. Also in life, there are people who sit by the sidelines, out of fear of

making a choice at all. But these same people also like to judge everyone else that actually rolls the dice from time to time. I tend to really dislike these people, because they act like judgmental authority but never took the risk to earn their stripes. But those people who sit by the sidelines judging everyone else already lost the game. Because the people who stepped up to take a risk are the ones who did more to take advantage of the opportunities of life. In the end, all of us have a time limit. There really are no 'safe' options for the long term. Life really is an opportunity, and all that fear manages to accomplish is to waste that opportunity.

4) One unique thing about being a human being is the ability to think and question. When it all comes down, every innovation or change for the better in life that humans have accomplished came from a thinking person who dared to question what was conventional. Every invention followed a similar process; someone thought that what was good was not good enough, and there had to be a better way. From the invention of the wheel all the way to internet solutions, someone thought deeply enough of something different… something new… that flew in the face of conventional thought. Some ideas were good, and others were pretty terrible, but life has a way of testing those out and rejecting the bad ideas.

There is also a similarity of people who think differently… Everyone who proposes something different will be met with the blow back of people who are used to conventional thought. It is most common for people to feel threatened by the highly difficult challenge of thinking that their original opinion can be updated as a result of new possibilities or information. So, every person who has the bravery to challenge what is conventional will be chastised. Every person who dares to make recognition that there may be a better way will be met with resistance. Anyone who starts a business will be met with some sort of resistance from those around them. Anyone who invents something new will be met with resistance from other people. Anyone who does not follow the orders of the family, the school, the church or the government will be met with embarrassment, ire, preaching, and sometimes even violence... from the people who are used to conventional ways of thinking and take the easy road to defend what is already conventional.

Many people I know do not fit in the conventional two-party system. I am part of this group. We open our eyes and see that there are many flaws in this system. We see that the people are not adequately represented. We see that the current system tramples independent thinkers. But when we speak up about it, we are told to sit down and shut up... that we must find a home on one side or the other. Because that is just the way it is, and it will never be changed. This defense of what is conventional is twofold: first, people don't like their beliefs to be challenged. It makes them pretty uncomfortable. And second, many people are lazy. So, the reaction a person gets when they step up to challenge conventional thinking is a pretty big wall.

It's just easier to do what other people think is normal. But if people like Nikola Tesla, Eli Whitney, and Jeff Bezos were lazy and did not have the bravery to think that the conventional ways of doing things were not cast in stone, we would not have the Radio, the Cotton Gin, or quick home delivery of just about everything at the touch of a button and the click of a mouse. But at some point, if independent thinkers are to be successful, they must successfully convince other people as to the merit of their idea, and how their idea would add value to their lives. For the fearless people who dare to challenge the two-party system, you must be able to do this, because it is much easier for people to hear your plans and laugh at you, because your plan challenges conventional thought.

Nothing worthwhile is easy. But David killed Goliath. Fictional as that story may be, it represents that human spark that what is seemingly insurmountable is possible with the right plan, the right innovation, and the right person to sell the innovation to others, knowing full well that they will meet with tremendous resistance, but have the power to overcome it. None of these successful people were lazy. They backed their new plan with tireless effort. A new and better way of running our country is possible. But we must get up off the couch and out into the world if it will ever become a reality. We must think of ourselves as salespeople, not educators. We must organize and follow through with our commitments. And once the successes are recognized, we must never fall back and take the easy road, for all would be lost. So, challenge convention. It's one of the greatest and most challenging benefits and responsibilities of being a human.

5) I love the idea of unity. For the American people to find those items that they can agree on and make recognition that there is agreement would be a good thing. To respect the people enough to let them live their chosen lives in peace

would result in unity. But sadly, this is rarely the goal of politicians in office. A politician that publicly states that they want to put you in prison because you have a plant in your pocket that relaxes you does not want unity. They want to control you. They claim to have good reasons, but it's really about control. A politician that publicly states that they want to put you in prison because you have a weapon in your home that you have decided is the most appropriate method of personal defense does not want unity. They want to control you. They claim to have good reasons, but it's really about control. A politician that publicly states that they want to forbid you from marrying in a way that they find immoral does not want unity. They want to control you. They claim to have good reasons, but it's really about control. A politician that states that they want to forbid you from driving your vehicle that you enjoy does not want unity. They want to control you.

They claim to have good reasons, but it's really about control. These are simple examples out of the myriad ways that a politician says they want unity, but also state that they want to stop you from doing something that you want to do. They also want to punish you for disobeying them. Mandatory is not a word used by anyone promoting voluntary unity. I am all for peace. I am all for unity. But actions speak louder than words. If unity is your goal, a crime must actually have a victim. Personal choices must remain just that... personal and a choice. The desire for unity is noble. But the more you want to tell people what they can and cannot do and threaten to punish people for non-compliance... well, that promotes anger and contempt... not peace and unity.

6) What is paranoia? One description states that, 'paranoia involves intense anxious or fearful feelings and thoughts often related to persecution, threat, or conspiracy'. While paranoia is a common component of mental illness, it seems more common than ever in the population at large. It should be pretty obvious to all that fear is the tool of politicians. It seems that fear and paranoia are strong motivating factors which result in people ceding control over their lives to someone else. The political persuasion merely changes the subjects that are used to scare people into political support. When a person ties in their personal fears with whatever information that is provided which grants them the ability to say, 'See! I was right!' it keeps the narrative alive. As the subject gains steam (more people afraid of the threat du jour) anyone who dares ask questions that may deflect from the narrative must be either stupid or evil, of course.

Those people must either be ridiculed or censored. Paranoia exists (in non-mental health situations) when a person is bombarded with information that is designed to ramp up their fears, thus sustaining the personal control they have ceded to the successful inciter of their fears. Paranoia is also a result of dishonest information from a formerly trusted source, such as government. Some examples of misinformation campaigns that lead to paranoia include...

A) When gun-related deaths are artificially inflated, it makes more people want to make laws banning guns.

B) When climate information is manipulated to prove

that global cooling is imminent (whoops, these people changed the narrative to warming a number of years later), this creates a paranoia. Anyone who dares to ask questions is met with, "How dare you!"

C) When the election is over and suddenly politicians who were all about scaring people into compliance for lockdowns are now changing their story that their cities and states must re-open, resulting in further mistrust of what was previously considered to be a trusted source of information (anyone who watched the CNN covid death clock would easily become obsessed with the invisible threat). Any time the government narrative is questioned, the name calling (and now censorship) is never far behind. The more obviously politically motivated the actions of government become, the less trust people will have in them. The less trust people have, the more paranoia will exist.

The tribalism doesn't really offset the paranoia. For example, people on the right are fearful that a pure Democrat-party-led government will do all it can to keep its power indefinitely. Some ways that have been suggested is the addition of several states such as DC, which will always provide two more democratic party Senators, thus tipping the balance in their favor indefinitely. Adding Supreme Court justices that are more political than defenders of the constitution is another way. Still another way is the destruction of the electoral college. So, while the left scares people into compliance with guns, climate change and covid, the right has paranoia of foreign and domestic enemies, drug users, and Democrats cheating the system to stay in control. My take from all this is that government is too big, and too involved in our lives, making otherwise healthy people more paranoid. Slashing the size and scope of government would go a long way to reducing paranoia in the population at large. It would not end irrational hatred of Presidents... that has gone on since the beginning of our constitutional republic. But it sure would make several hundred million people mellow out quite a bit, and live happier lives.

7) The societal organizer is a person who views society as something they can unilaterally control and coordinate. It does not enter their mind that the human beings that would be affected by their classification, regulation and construction could be harmed as a result. They believe so deeply that they are correct, that those harmed are just broken eggs in an omelet, and a cost of implementing their grand scheme. The egocentricity of their plans and goals should scare all of us to death... but instead, we elect them to offices, which grant them the power to bring their plans to fruition. We advocate for them because they share our precious political initial.

Most people are not willing to be the broken egg, and I cannot blame them. Some people, especially socialists, condescend to the argument in favor of individual freedom, because it becomes a monkey wrench in their plans or goals, or gets in the way of addressing whatever they are afraid of. I wonder how they would feel if they were the egg that was about to be broken so that someone else could achieve their goal instead. Freedom is something to be fought for and thankful for, not pushed out of the way in order to implement your selfish desires.

8) I encourage you to read this short passage about the progression to central control under Josef Stalin in the USSR. You may recognize this exact thing happening here at home, if you have been listening to members of the US Congress and the US Senate who have identified the USA as an oligarchy with their frustration in their inability to participate and do their jobs properly. All of us must be mindful of history in order to stop it from repeating. Please open your eyes and get meaningfully involved, or there is a very good chance that we will experience this here at home. Don't fool yourself to believe that we are any different, and somehow we are impervious to repeating these same mistakes.

The passage: 'This tradition of tight centralization, with decision-making concentrated at the highest party levels, reached new dimensions under Joseph Stalin. As many of these archival documents show, there was little input from below. The party elite determined the goals of the state and the means of achieving them in almost complete isolation from the people. They believed that the interests of the individual were to be sacrificed to those of the state, which was advancing a sacred social task. Stalin's "revolution from above" sought to build socialism by means of forced collectivization and industrialization, programs that entailed tremendous human suffering and loss of life.' If you don't want this for your future generations, you had better act now.

9) If only the GOP wasn't so anti-freedom. Having observed the left over the last ten years or so, I now understand how socialist countries always became brutal dictatorships. A debate with a leftist will go one of two ways: A) They will condescend to you because of their self-proclaimed superior intelligence; or B) they will scream bloody murder at you and call you every name in the book. So. if that is the personality that clamors to turn our Republic into a 'socialist democracy' (eventually better known as a brutal dictatorship), the leadership would follow these personality traits. Vladimir Lenin spouted all the peaceful sounding anti-capitalist drivel we now hear from the AOC/Sanders group. That became the violent Union of Soviet SOCIALIST Republics. Fidel Castro was the same revolutionary, as was Hugo Chavez, Adolf Hitler, Mao Tse Tung, and every other Socialist in history. Socialism really breaks down to one concept: control all the people. SOCIAList. The absolute opposite of INDIVIDUAList. This is why you encounter such sheer anger when you disagree with a socialist. They want to control you with every fiber of their being, and anyone who stands in their way is their mortal enemy. So yes, the USA has implemented some socialist policies in the last one hundred years. But to go full USSR is not something I can stand by and quietly accept. After all, how many happy people (other than the Politburo) lived in the USSR? No thanks.

10) If one group of scientists disagree with your preferred group of scientists, is that first group science deniers? I have been thinking about this subject, because there is so much disagreement out there about whatever the threats du jour

happen to be. It seems that this all comes down to more group think and mob rule. How many of you have experienced people making fun of you for asking questions? Have your questions been met with condescension? Are you abruptly shut down with 'the science is settled'? Science is a moving issue. What was established fact in the past was commonly dis-proven. Does anyone think about the whole 'theory vs theorem' definition anymore? I don't remember seeing this in recent years.

Most of my university education was as a biology major. When new ideas were explained to us forty years ago, the political bent of today was simply not there. New concepts entered the discussion and those were theories. If those theories were proven to be factual, they became theorems. Today, there are no theories or theorems. Just panic-driven manipulations of scary things that require that your wallet is drained, your careers are interrupted, and that you must vote for certain politicians in order to save the children… no questions asked.

During my college days, it was more about trying to find solutions. It was finding new ways of thinking and new technologies designed to fight diseases and invent more reliable methods to solving problems. No one ever argued if the science was settled. They did honest research. There was little or no political motivation. Sure, studies were designed by the holder of the theory with hopes of proving that their theory was correct, but if it was wrong, it was wrong. Humanity has learned tremendous lessons from the study of science. Many problems have been solved. Horrible diseases have been eradicated. I am sad to see what has become of the public perception and government manipulation of the field of science. It seems that once money and politics enter any realm, credibility is damaged. It's such a shame...

11) When a politician makes a statement that you don't 'need' something, it means they want to make laws telling you that you can't have it if you want it. It means that they think they know better than you do about how you should live your life. It means prohibition or regulation. It means you can get arrested, fined, jailed, or killed if you have it, or fail to pay the government if you choose to possess it. Don't fall for this innocuous sounding lead-in. What I need is none of your damn business. If you say this is a free country, walk the walk... don't just talk the talk.

12) How can a group of people who do not share your reality sit in a room and decide what's best for you? What if these people are constantly being influenced by lobbyists who are paid to benefit their clients? What if these people also must pay back the people who helped them get elected by their actions while in office? What if these people did not have good ideas in the first place? What if these people have personal prejudices from their own life experiences and teachings that actually make them do bad things for the people who are affected by their actions?

   In the end, few people would care about what these people sitting in a room actually do, if their actions did not have a meaningful impact on their lives, their families' lives, their ability to support themselves, their personal freedom and their pursuit of happiness. To make matters worse, these people in a room make rules for everyone to follow, or be punished for non-compliance, regardless of their circumstances, which can vary tremendously depending on where they live in this large and diverse country. For some people who think more about what these people actually do, instead of what precious initial they have by their names, this is why they get so upset by who is elected to be in this room. So next time around, how about not trying to shame people for trying to build and support something different, especially if their goal is to reduce the impact of these few people in a room over everyone in the entire country.

13) To recap: you cannot have most jobs unless you pay the government. You cannot drive your vehicle unless you pay the government. You cannot build your home unless you pay the government. You could not consume cannabis until the government got a share of the profits. You could not gamble until the government got a share of the profits. Actually, there are very few activities out there that don't require a payment to the government... unless they are illegal. I guess that when you get to make the laws, you make them all in your own best interest. This is why the country was designed with very minimal government that was supposed to be mistrusted by the people. Too bad there was always a good reason to look the other way and let it get out of hand.

14) 2016 – Democrats: "Waaaaaa! They cheated!" (Continues into 2017, 2018, 2019, 2020 with Russian probes, impeachments, growing the National Popular Vote compact and constant editorial reporting replacing news

reporting...). 2016 – Republicans: "We won? – cool! Looks like the media was lying all along!" 2020 – Democrats: (Spikes the ball, laughing...) "You will eat it and you will like it, now go sit in the corner and shut up. Now that we won, it's time for unity!" 2020 – Republicans: "Something doesn't seem right... I think we need to look into this before moving on." 2020 – Democrats again: "How dare you question the process! It has been perfect all along! Nothing to see here... I said sit down and shut up!"

This is why politics is both maddening and compelling all rolled up into one...

15) If you want to keep the money you earned from your labor, you are not selfish. No need to let people with a political motive shame you for this... especially the people that want that stolen money given to them. When you were a kid, and you earned $5 for mowing the lawn, you did not expect to receive $3 and have the other $2 sent to the government to bomb people under the guise of helping the poor. If you donate some of the money you earned from your labor, you have done so voluntarily; you are generous because you did so without being forced. If you donate your time and effort to helping others without pay, you are someone I am proud of and grateful for. It is people like you that truly care about helping others... even if you did not have your pay taken away from you and given to the government without your consent. Don't confuse selfishness with political manipulation. Give if yourself freely. When you make this choice, the benefit of your action goes where you intend for it to go... it is pure of heart and does not support bombing innocent people around the

world.

16) For most people, their reality dictates what is important to them. If they can't cover their cost of living and feel that they have tried their best, they either give up or look for solutions. It is true that millennials make up the largest percentage of the workforce in the USA, and only control 4.6% of the wealth. This is a big problem. When you scold them for complaining and tell them to try harder, it only makes many of them feel more desperate... and angry at the few people who hold all the cards. The consensus among the youth of today is that they have little hope of building a life that is similar to their predecessors, who they also blame for the conditions that they currently face.

They want to level the playing field. They see that the only way to accomplish this is to take the money away from the rich people that they perceive are taking advantage of them. They listen to left-leaning media which censors out information that might make them see the whole picture. They went to government-controlled schools which made them see that government is the best answer to address all problems. So, of course, they advocate for more government to take away the wealth from other people and spread it around to everyone. By now, most of you know how I feel about government overreach.

Unless a person enters the main stage who can effectively help out young people to comprehend that the insurmountable hurdles to their success are created mostly by government, this country will continue to build more government, which costs more money, which creates more barriers to innovation, which kills more and more small businesses, which increases the national debt, which makes these people pay a higher portion of their earnings in taxes to service the interest on this debt, which creates more laws which results in the arrest and imprisonment of more people, which creates more wars, which makes housing more expensive, which makes their lives more and more difficult instead of solving the problems that are plaguing our younger generations. There is beauty in simplicity. If our future generations are to have better and more satisfying lives, they need to be exposed to the simple realities that makes this possible. The bottom line is really simple. The fewer barriers that are in the way of their success, the more people will become successful. This is what they need to hear, instead of put downs and scolding.

17) The following is a constant: big cities vote Democrat. Everywhere else votes Republican. This makes sense. Big cities are more reliant on societal infrastructure, and rural areas are more self-reliant. This is completely understandable. The reason for the anger is this: the federal government has become all-encompassing. It has created laws, regulations and other restrictions that are more applicable in the big cities but apply to the entire country. One peaceful solution is to reduce the federal government to once again provide for the common defense, resolve high-level disputes, and ensure the liberty of the individual. The states would still have the problem of being controlled by the big cities within the states, however. But how can we achieve this when the big cities overwhelmingly clamor for a bigger federal government, and control their entire states as well?

Answer: we can't. The big cities would never allow it. Here is my solution to this problem. It would take a well-organized restructuring of the political system via constitutional amendment, that I call the 'live and let live amendment'. The live and let live amendment allows big cities to build their infrastructures the way they want, and areas outside the big cities to opt out from big city rule, kind of like the old 'home rule' constitutional amendments in state constitutions. If the 'live and let live amendment' were to become the law of the land, there would be no more discussion of civil war, no more 'R vs. D' hatred, and peace would once again prevail here in the good old USA.

18) The United States was created as a Constitutional Republic. Why is this fact so important? Because the reason for the design was to protect the rights of the individual. I believe that every person matters. As the constitutional republic is dismantled brick by brick, and with it the constitution, the right of the individual to be an individual is dismantled with it. As the constitutional republic is replaced with the mob rule of pure democracy, one person becomes meaningless if that person dares to differ from the iron fist of the state. Public opinion and outrage changes issues and attitudes quite often. Politicians typically cater to the desires of the public, because that is how they keep their jobs. But once the state controls the schools and the media, the dynamic shifts to the state controlling public opinion.

When the state controls public opinion, the idea of the people controlling the state is dead. People do as they are told to back the desires of the state in their votes. We already see this in California, where the elections are Democrat vs.

Democrat. So then why would the state want this? Because the state believes it knows best for all of you about how you should live your lives. It thinks that you are not capable of making your own decisions. If the state can control every aspect of your life, it solidifies its power. And in the end, power is what the state craves. The National Popular Vote movement is another tool in the arsenal of the movement toward socialism to reduce the voice of the individual, and replace it with the voice of the mob which has been programmed by the state to comply. The National Popular Vote movement is one more nail in the coffin of the USA being a constitutional republic. The National Popular Vote movement is duct tape over your mouth. The National Popular Vote movement must be defeated at all costs.

19) People are only willing to vote for higher taxes for other people to pay.

So, let's say you earned $400k per year. If your income taxes cost you $240k of that, and you still had to pay; employee social security tax (your employer pays the other half); employee Medicare tax (your employer pays the other half); property taxes road toll charges; state sales tax; driver's license renewal fee; TV cable/satellite fees & taxes; federal telephone surtax, excise tax and universal surcharge; state telephone excise tax and surcharge; telephone minimum usage and recurring/nonrecurring charges tax; gas/electric bill fees & taxes; water/sewer fees & taxes; cigarette tax; alcohol tax; federal gasoline tax; state gasoline tax; local gasoline tax; federal inheritance tax; state inheritance tax; gift tax; bridge toll charges; marriage license; hunting license; fishing license; bike license fee;

dog permit/license; state park permit; watercraft registration & licensing fees; sports stadium tax; bike/nature trail permit; court case filing fee; retirement account early withdrawal penalty; individual health insurance mandate tax; hotel stay tax; plastic surgery surcharge; soda/fatty-food tax; air transportation tax; electronic transmission of tax return fees; passport application/renewal fee; luxury & gas-guzzler car taxes; new car surcharge; license plate and car ownership transfer taxes; yacht and luxury boat taxes; jewelry taxes & surcharges; state/local school tax; recreational vehicle tax; special assessments for road repairs or construction; gun ownership permit; kiddie tax (IRS form 8615); fuel gross receipts tax; waste management tax; oil and gas assessment tax; use taxes (on out-of-state purchase); IRA rollover tax/withdrawal penalties; tax on non-qualified health saving account distributions; federal unemployment tax; state unemployment tax; business registration renewal tax; worker's compensation tax; tax on imported/exported goods; oil storage/inspection fees; employer health insurance mandate tax; excise tax on charitable hospitals (page 2001/Sec. 9007 of Obamacare); tax on innovator drug companies (Page 2010/Sec. 9008 of Obamacare); tax on medical device manufacturers (Page 2020/Sec. 9009 of Obamacare); tax on health insurers (Page 2026/Sec. 9010 of Obamacare); excise tax on comprehensive health insurance plans, i.e. 'Cadillac' plans; tax on indoor tanning services; utility users tax; internet transaction fee (passed in California; being considered in other states and at federal level); professional license fee (accountants, lawyers, barbers, dentists, plumbers, etc.); franchise business tax;

tourism and concession license fee; wiring inspection fees; household employment tax; biodiesel fuel tax; FDIC tax (insurance premium on bank deposits); electronic waste recycling fee; hazardous material disposal fee; food & beverage license fee; estimated income tax underpayment penalty; building/construction permit; zoning permit; fire inspection fee; well permit tax; sales and use tax seller's permit; commercial driver's license fee; bank ATM transaction tax; occupation taxes and fees (annual charges required for a host of professions), that might leave you about $1.98 for food, housing, utilities, etc. You can almost buy a lottery ticket with that... But wait, you would lose your lottery winnings too. But what would you get for the $399,998.02? Bombs... lots of bombs...

20) This is why it is such a challenge to overcome the two-party system in the USA. The two-party system is taught to our kids in school. Citizenship exams include the question to name the two political parties in the USA. The Democratic Party controls most of the television news and newspapers in the USA, and the Republican Party controls what is not controlled by the Democratic Party. Political polls exclude third party candidates on the same line as the Republican and Democratic candidate, and the debate participants are largely selected by polling results which exclude everyone other than the Democrat and the Republican. The people of this country are indoctrinated in every way, shape and form by schools, media, and government that there are only two parties from the time they begin to talk.

This is why you run into so many apologists for the

two-party system. It takes something super powerful to make the people re-think that there are more soft drinks than just Coke and Pepsi. The same people that control the thoughts of Americans also try to teach them to blame the other party for everything that is wrong, while defending the malevolent actions of members of their party. When it all comes down to it, fear is what controls the people that are interested in getting behind a better option, and that fear is hard to overcome. When you are surrounded by others who tell you that your candidate cannot win, and that you are wasting your vote by voting for someone other than the candidate that they support, it takes a special bravery not to succumb to that programming at the ballot box. Most people still have that little inkling in the back of their minds that the lesser of two evils is still better, and that the lesser of two evils is somehow not evil, which is ridiculous.

21) When California and Montana have to live by the same rules, one of them will be miserable. The job of the US President was supposed to be commander in chief of the US military and head of state in foreign relations, reporting back to the people at least once per year. Because of the failure of our elected representatives over the last century (give or take) to not only write legislation that satisfies the required minority protections of the constitution, and instead to completely trample it, the power of the Presidency has mushroomed to proportions where their edicts affect everyone in the country.

If the federal government was forced to stay within its original constraints over the years, or is forced to revert to its original role and thereby granting more power to the states and localities, there would not be anywhere near the present anger over this presidential race. Instead of attacking the divisive people nominated by the Democratic and Republican party for these offices, it would be more effective to keep your eyes the on big picture. Reducing the size and scope of the federal government would make it so that it becomes less important who wins the federal elections. Unfortunately, none of these candidates will reduce the size or the scope of the federal government, so working from the ground up is the only way to move things in the right direction. There is no need for half of the country to always be miserable.

22) What is a central planner? It's a person that is so sure that they are so much smarter than you are that they want to make laws which force you to comply with their plans for you, even when their imposed requirements are completely the opposite of your own life plan. A central planner claims ownership over your life. There is a place where societal requirements and the greater good is determined by other people. It's a place where compliance is required and the penalties for non-compliance are severe. It's a place where everyone is forced to receive the same government-imposed indoctrination and place society over the individual. That place is North Korea. Sorry central planners, but moving the USA to become even more like North Korea seems to me like a serious violation of our responsibility as Americans, and our role as stewards of the Constitution. Some may think that the desire for individual freedom for all is a joke, but I am sure that the myriad people who lost their lives for the sole purpose of fighting

government tyranny in the revolutionary war would beg to differ. And by the way... no one knows better than you do about how you should live your life. Especially central planners with a thirst for power.

23) After George Washington's death, Thomas Jefferson described him in unforgettable terms. 'His mind was great and powerful,' he was 'incapable of fear,' and his 'integrity was most pure'. Washington was 'in every sense of the words, a good and a great man'. How would today's government describe George Washington if he lived two hundred years later? A subversive? A radical? A scofflaw? If a government of the people and by the people is to be successful, it must not describe people who question its actions and motives as an enemy. A person who stands up for the original purpose of this country is a patriot, especially if they argue with what is conventionally accepted due to apathy and laziness. Tyranny will always happen when a government is unchecked. The battle for freedom is ongoing, and always will be.

24) How many of you are searching for the key that unlocks the door to a better life? I have been searching for the key that unlocks the door to peace and prosperity for everyone who wants it. What seems clear to me is that many people have the skills to do great things. So then why are the majority of people in this country struggling? Why are so many people angry? Why are so many people suffering? In short, we reap what we sow. The decisions that we make can end up with positive results, negative results, or no results at all. Some things are out of our control. Sometimes

there are negative occurrences that are unavoidable. Occasionally, there are positive surprises as well.

When large numbers of people get together and form a society, rules are an inevitability. After all, killing, assaulting and stealing should not be acceptable in any society. It's not hard for people to agree that these are bad. But people are complex creatures that have a need to be productive, and it's rare for people to leave well enough alone. I have seen people purchase successful restaurants, and then change the menu. Their desire to be productive ended up destroying their investment. When people create a body for the purpose of making rules, they too need to feel productive. The need for productivity universally overrules the correct choice of leaving well enough alone. Today, the sheer number of rules and the zero-tolerance enforcement has created an environment in which what should be positive decisions yield negative results. This is the key that we have been looking for. This rule-making body just kept on making rules and enforcing them with violence. And with so many people enforcing so many rules, their need to be productive ended up making every person a potential victim.

Now it is time to unlock the door to peace and prosperity for everyone who wants it. The way to accomplish this task is for rule making bodies to use that need for productivity by dismantling the spider web that they created. My vision of government is pretty simple. Three words: 'help, don't hurt'. Let's spend the next twenty years concentrating on repealing laws and regulations that create victims out of people that never hurt anyone else. That is the key which unlocks the door to peace and prosperity for everyone who is willing to do the work to achieve their dreams. When we sow seeds for a beautiful garden, and people in positions of authority mow down the garden because it was not planted in compliance with their vision and strict rules for gardening, the garden is destroyed. Who wins when your garden is destroyed? One might say the people who destroyed it won, because their action helped them keep their jobs for one more day. But in the end, that garden could have fed them and their families when they needed it had they not destroyed it. When reaping positive results is constantly blocked as a result of too many rules and heavy-handed enforcement of those rules, you can never reap what you planned to sow. Too many rules ends freedom... and freedom matters if we have goals and dreams and have hope to achieve them...

25) Capitalism is far from perfect. People with more money than other people do indeed take advantage of those with meager incomes. Socialism is worse, because it sees people more as cogs in a wheel than people with individual drive and desire. Communism is even worse, because it amplifies socialism. The real bottom line is this: people want to feel secure. But they also want to explore their potential and follow their own dreams. When a socialist or communist government is installed, it wants the power to stop people from following their dreams. While capitalism has its down side, if people can no longer follow their dreams, they are not living this life to its fullest. So, capitalism sucks for those who are not willing to make efforts. But socialism and communism makes it impossible for people willing to make the effort to follow their dreams. My advice? Never let

anyone stop you from following your dreams. Socialism and communism may be appealing for some at the moment... but it's just not worth the tradeoff.

26) Have you been at a point in your life when you felt helpless? How about hopeless? Most of us have experienced times in our lives where we had these feelings. What percentage of the people are innovative enough to come up with creative solutions to their seemingly insurmountable problems? Those educated in government schools are taught to look no further than government to solve them. Money doesn't grow on trees, and the long-term shortage of money has resulted in countless suicides, and more pain than most people realize. Millions of people do not have faith in their ability to find creative solutions to the economic problems that they face today. They see the cost of housing as nearly unattainable, and many people are one paycheck away from being homeless.

Many people are aware of the fact that if they were to become seriously ill, they may not be able to afford lifesaving medical care... especially those with Obamacare basic insurance policies. Most people have only been exposed to one way to address this problem... forcefully taking the assets of highly successful people in order to provide for their necessities. At the same time, these people have pride. They feel the need to justify their proposals to rob the rich and give to themselves. So, they villainize successful people. It doesn't feel as bad to steal from bad people that 'don't deserve what they have in the first place'. I understand envy and jealousy. How much easier would life be if you were born into immense wealth? You would not be facing the problems that you do right now... with no money while at the same time people are threatening you to pay them what you do not have.

It would be wonderful not to be faced with this endless cycle of being required to pay money that you can't afford to pay. So they devise strategies to use the force of government to take away from those that have and give to those that do not. I suppose that using government is easier for them, because they don't need their own mask and gun... government has plenty of guns and is not afraid to use them in the pursuit of forcing the people to obey. Ladies and gentlemen, this is the foundation that has allowed for American citizens to clamor for socialism by the millions. They want to build a government that robs from the rich and gives to the poor. They want Robin Hood. But I must warn you. When people are granted power over other people, they are not Robin Hood. They are not altruistic. Power is a drug. Power is a disease.

Those who desire power always want more and more power. When you agree to elevate government to the position of Robin Hood, it evolves to killing those who disagree. If you need any proof, look at the 20th century experience with socialism, and the over one hundred million people killed in wars or by dictators desirous of eliminating threats to their power. I ask you all to make recognition of these facts: A) Government overreach is why housing is so expensive; B) Government overreach is the reason why medical care is out of reach; C) Government overreach is the reason why higher education is unattainable for many. So... knowing all this... why would you support giving government more of your earnings and more power when the simple act of slashing the size and scope of government would give you back your ability to cover these expenses on your own, within your own budget?

27) Some people really hate large corporations, and want more government to control them and limit their ability to make profits. Some people really hate government, and want the corporations left alone to compete, and make better and more affordable products. The reality of this conflict is that small businesses are the most innovative and fast moving, and are constantly being crushed under the weight of both of these types of entities. Why else would large corporations do all they can to control politicians, and thereby control government? It sustains them, while killing small business competitors who move more quickly and are more innovative. The irony is that people who clamor for more regulation because they hate the large corporations are actually helping the large corporations by eliminating smaller and more nimble competition... the family business.

28) Some local governments are now going after dollar stores. If one steps back to take in the entire picture, they will see that the activities of government are responsible for the suffering of many hard-working people. It is all too common that a person builds their lives, becomes prosperous, and loses the fruits of their labor due to the self-serving actions of government. On their way down, they were forced to utilize more desperate or unpleasant measures in order to survive. But government eliminates

them one by one. Payday loans. Hunger assistance without permits. Offering free temporary housing in your own home. Now dollar stores. Once on the street with no remaining means of survival, your tents are slashed and the remaining community that has not been destroyed wants to remove you from their sight because they see you as a nuisance. If you go through the appropriate motions, there may be some assistance for you... from the same government that destroyed you. It was said that government will break your leg and if you ask nicely they will give you a crutch, then expect to be praised for being there for you.

29) MLK fought for freedom. It was obvious to his oppressed followers (and everybody else) that they were not free. MLK was a very important figure in US history, and I am grateful for his efforts. Sadly, it is more difficult for the masses today to realize that they are not free, because they are taught that they live in a free country. This country needs a modern MLK for those who have been programmed by the tyrants to believe that they are free. But I ask you... would a free country have the highest incarceration rate of its citizens in the entire world? Would a free country make every personal choice either regulated, taxed, or illegal? Now some politicians are coming for the first and second amendments, and their followers cheer them on. If those are removed, will you still believe what you are taught about freedom, or will you stand up and do something about it?

30) Desperate people do desperate things. Morality is always trumped by necessity. When a person or their family is starving, stealing is a better choice than dying... even

among the most moral people. Especially over the last forty years, government intervention has made housing unaffordable... because of too many rules. Health care is out of reach... because of too many rules. Higher education is out of the question... because of too many rules. Government loves to punish people who do not obey its rules. But a government which controls the schools teaches that compliance with government edicts is a good thing because we are lucky to live with all of our freedoms. The people are not instructed that government could ever be the problem.

Enter 2020. The people know that they have a problem. Housing costs take up the lion's share of most people's income. Obamacare has resulted in the cost of health coverage to be in the same ballpark with rents or mortgages for older people... and the deductible is three months' pay. Education is a pipe dream for many who want careers that require it. Forty years ago, as the USSR was suffering from a severe shortage of basic goods as most socialist countries have experienced, very few Americans would have wanted to embrace their system. Sure, some people's reverence to the state supported all of the tyranny that the state could muster as they closely monitored the people... arresting and incarcerating as many people as possible that did not bow to the will of the state (the war on drugs is a great example of this).

But today, people are desperate. So, they advocate for the policies of the old USSR, Venezuela, Cuba, North Korea, etc. They cite Sweden, which is not a socialist country and had to move away from socialist policies in order to avoid collapse. They look to the very institution that made their financial lives impossible to fix the problem that it created, and believe that government would never take advantage of the people and an oppressive ruling class would never happen here. They fail to recognize that a massive reduction in government attacks against the activities of private citizens would repair the problem quickly, and without doubling or tripling the national debt for future generations to deal with. Most desperate decisions have long term consequences.

31) Government makes laws and regulations which create homeless and hungry people due to excess enforcement of laws and regulations which create criminals out of people that did not harm anyone else. Government cronyism chooses winners and losers which put hard working people out of work. Industries are destroyed and jobs lost as a result of new government forced prohibitions. Government also makes laws which stand in the way of private citizens who want to assist people in need without permits or other types of government control. This assistance must also comply with restrictive zoning laws. These laws stand in the way of helping people that are homeless or hungry due to many reasons, but many due to the activities of government. Government also arrests and/or fines people who feed hungry people or house homeless people outside of government control. Government has also destroyed food for the hungry due to non-compliance with their laws and regulations. So... sure... give more money to government to solve this problem. The right answer? Volunteer to help, and band together to end government prohibitions to helping those in need, and ending laws and regulations

which make innocent, hardworking people end up homeless and/or hungry.

32) A brief discussion of 'trust'. When trust is violated with respect to one issue, the violator of trust has lost trust. If our trust is violated enough times by one person or entity, it is natural to question or disbelieve everything that person or entity has told us. In contract law, that concept is addressed with a 'severability clause', which basically says that if one part of the contract does not comply with applicable law, the rest of the contract remains enforceable. If government communications had a 'severability clause', the 10% or so of completely honest communications would be protected, even though 90% of what we are told has some level of dishonesty. But there can be no severability clause when it comes to credibility of communications. This is why thinking people become contrarian and entertain alternative explanations for many current and historical events and situations.

The conventional tales we are told in our schools and history books are the generally accepted explanations. But just because these explanations are taught to us in our schools, they are not automatically accurate. This lack of consistent credibility is a big problem. Many people are more certain of what they have surmised or deduced from their own independent study of historical events than the conventional story and will argue their views with passion. Are they right? I am not sure. Are they wrong? I am not sure. But I also tend to disbelieve that which is communicated to me by those in power over the people. I am not a proponent of many laws which create criminals, or which remove freedom, unless the action creates a victim. But it seems to me that when a source such as government which should be trustworthy lies to the public, there should be a penalty. But there is no penalty when government agencies publicly lie to the people or omit key facts in their communications. Why is there no penalty for disseminating misinformation by government entities? Because government entities have the ability to make laws, and they will never make a law which could harm themselves. This is reason #757392 why government must be reduced.

33) Politics are contentious because what politicians do affects you. Some politicians want to take your money and spend it on things that make their donors wealthier. Some politicians want to take your money and build more enforcement infrastructure against you. Some politicians want to make something you enjoy illegal. Some politicians want to bomb other countries. Some politicians want to force you to carry out those bombings. Some politicians believe so strongly in government that they ban your acts of kindness without government permission. Some politicians want to destroy your business. Some politicians want to take more of your money to give to other countries after they take a cut for themselves. Maybe we all should get out of the partisan rut and support politicians that want to cut government and make you free and financially healthy instead.

34) California is really a symptom of a much larger problem. When the United States of America was born, and

the bill of rights became the backbone of the land, the framers of the constitution included the 10th Amendment. As each state was really like its own country, pooling their resources for defense, the 10th Amendment was there to protect the autonomy of each state against an overbearing federal government. But as governments typically do... it found a way around the 10th Amendment (and all the others but the 3rd) and is now massive and attempts to control the lives of all of the people, in all states (if you need an example of this, you need to look no further than the war on drugs).

Back to the discussion on California. California leans very socialist, and if that is what Californians want, good for them. But with a federal government which controls us all, and the massive population numbers in California, attempts to control the federal government by socialists in California now means that there is a real attempt to turn the entire country socialist. The National Popular Vote compact (NPV) is evidence of these attempts, and in some states they are working. If California chooses President, it will do all it can to turn the rest of the country into California. I think it's time to recognize two foundational resolutions: First, if California wants to live like Venezuela, they have that right, and second, they should not have the right to make the rest of us live like Venezuela. The only way to allow this to happen is to shrink the size and scope of the federal government to original constitutional levels, and reinstate the bill of rights to the original intent of those who drafted it.

35) The real argument between the people is what takes

precedence, the good of society or the rights of the individual to exercise free will? It seems to me that society is most benefited by the individual having the right to exercise free will. When laws are created which are designed to benefit society over the individual, this is nothing more than mob rule. Mobs don't always try to force good things. If you have any doubts about this statement, you need not look beyond the Nazi regime, the KKK, Stalin's Russia, Castro's Cuba, Mao's China, or the likely results of Bernie Sanders, Elizabeth Warren, or Alexandria Ocasio-Cortes.

It's easy to paint a pretty picture of a benevolent dictator, but when that benevolent dictator is replaced with a not-so benevolent one (which always happens), the rainbows and unicorns are replaced with violence and heavy-handed control. But what I find most puzzling is that the people on the right who advocate for individual freedom also support the violence and heavy-handed control of the police state and military assaults on the innocent people of other countries. These same people clamor for balanced budgets but support a leader (who shares their precious initial) who continues to increase the deficit and debt. This is why the two-party system is more than a failure... it's an abomination. But sure... keep screaming about which 'side' is worse instead of supporting those who would actually work toward freedom for the individual.

It has worked so well that the cost of our basic needs is out of reach, millions of people in this country are homeless and or hungry, education is for the rich, health care is good, bad or non-existent depending on your economic situation, but there is plenty of our money to send to other countries, wage endless wars, and to arrest and incarcerate millions of people for personal choices that harmed no one… and there is no end in sight to this strategy if you listen to the current rhetoric from both sides. This is what your precious two-party system built… a police state which takes away your money to support violence and oppression, yet operates under the guise of freedom.

36) Human induced climate change: A Trojan horse. Politicians have long known that the subservient class responds to fear. This fear is utilized by clever politicians to trick people into supporting them over their competitor who does not claim to defend you against whatever it is that is supposed to scare you. For as long as I can remember, fear has been thrust on the people. I remember 'duck and cover drills' as far back as the first grade, where ducking under the desk and covering the eyes and the back of the neck would somehow serve to protect us from being liquidated in a nuclear attack. We were taught that marijuana was the 'devil's lettuce' (later exposed as Nixon's political trick against his detractors) as the taxed and regulated alcohol flowed freely… We were told to 'love it or leave it' if we dared to speak to the fact that the Vietnam war was unjust and unwinnable.

We were taught to fear communists. We were taught to fear beatniks and hippies. We were taught to fear anything that was different than we were. Fear is a political tool. So, when one group embraces the new scare tactic and uses it to gain power and control… and your money… most people still fall for it. Acid rain. Hole in the ozone. Global Warming. Climate change. All with the support of scientists. Need I remind you that scientists also buried the dangers of sugar and blamed fat for all our ills. I have learned to take politically motivated scare tactics and divide them by ten as a rule, to figure out what is the real impact of whatever they want us to be afraid of today.

If you really want to be scared... consider this: if they sell you on the idea that climate change is human induced, they own you. You will support everything they want to do because you love your children and the generations to come. If they gain power by scaring you, guess what? The Trojan Horse will empty out and the people in charge will look more like Josef Stalin than the Little Mermaid. Fear should always be something to avoid when making political choices. There will always be plenty of fear to go around, so if you really want the best for your children and the generations to come... think for yourself, think globally... and if they have something to gain by trying to scare you... look in a different direction.

Unless you are the climate scientist that performs an independent analysis of the data and arrives at a conclusion, this comes down to who to believe. There are some scientists who believe that all of these changes are a result of the activities of humans, and there are others who believe that this is purely natural and cyclical. Some scientists have defined these changes as either no change at all, some have defined it as mild, moderate or severe. A consensus (the 97% debacle) was circulated by government agencies and this was later proven to be a complete lie. So, ultimately, this comes down to who to believe. My usual analysis bases itself on who has the most to gain from people accepting their hypotheses. Unfortunately, the most transparently power grabby are the strongest proponents of the Chicken Little argument.

They are manipulating our youth with the most extreme argument, and they are doing what they do... accepting this one argument hook, line and sinker, and trying to take over the political arena with all the outrage and panic that would bring Alexandria Ocasio-Cortez and her ilk firmly in control of this country. There are kids committing to never having kids unless the power is handed to this group of totalitarian dictators. And why? Because they believe one person's opinion over another person's opinion. If I step back and look at this situation as impartially as I can, I would guess that there is some truth to the assertion that human activities have impacted our climate in some way, shape or form. I also see that the panic was orchestrated in order to result in a political takeover.

So, the problem as I see it is to actually obtain real information, provided by people that have nothing to gain or lose in the presentation of their findings. Unfortunately, in this politically-charged country it seems that we would only find this credible source in a different country. So I would not recommend burying our heads in the sand any more than I would recommend handing the keys to the country to people that would lead us down the road to another USSR. I would recommend private research and analysis to find the unvarnished truth of the situation, and to disseminate a solution (if one is ultimately needed) that people can get behind, without the violence and fraud that are constant components of any government solution.

37) The founding fathers of the USA incorporated a system

of checks and balances in their structure for the federal government. This was for the purpose of preventing any person or entity in government to gain too much power and to rule with impunity... unchecked. Today, checks and balances are largely a thing of the past. Sure, the Supreme Court may overrule legislation, or legislators may overrule a Supreme Court decision with a Constitutional Amendment... but looking at local law enforcement and regulators, there is the illusion of checks and balances. But when a law enforcement officer breaches their duty or kills a nonthreatening, innocent person, they are typically exonerated.

When a regulator wields unreasonable punishment over a business, they do so unfettered for the most part. I have even heard of a small business that prevailed in an administrative law court, and the regulators ignored the ruling of the court... right here in Colorado. Have you ever met a prosecutor? Although a prosecutor is charged with discovering the truth, the vast majority of prosecutors only care about winning, because winning is what furthers their compensation, promotions and political careers. No matter what excuse you may have for the actions of these government personnel, the ability to act against the public with no real checks or balances destroys the concept of a government of the people, by the people and for the people. This type of action is what creates the chasm between the people and the very government that we are charged to control. And to make matters worse... you have to pay for these attacks against you when you pay your taxes. This is one of many reasons it is time for a real political change away from the two-party system which allowed this to happen.

38) People are angry about politics. The overblown size and scope of the federal government is the reason why. What started as a vehicle to pool the resources of the states for a common defense now controls every breath you take. It controls every bite you consume. It controls every drug you utilize for your own health. It has studied all your cell phone calls. It controls your children's education. It has made so many regulations that only large corporations can keep up with them. It has made banking unavailable to your legal business if it didn't like what you do. It takes a large portion of the money that you work to earn and uses it to monitor, control and punish you for non-compliance with their edicts that are not the edicts of a free country.

The realities of life in our fifty states are different. But the federal government acts to make life in our fifty different states the same... standardized. The anger is due to the fact that the fight for control of the federal government is a fight to control us all, which was not the purpose of creating a federal government in the first place. The federal government must go through a long period of reduction if the people are ever to have a chance at freedom, satisfaction and a chance to live to our potential as individuals. We the people of the United States of America need to reclaim our independence... one person at a time... and that time is now.

39) There is a dichotomy of views in our country about the effectiveness and end result of laws. Once again, there are extremes, but these extremes are inconsistent. The left

believes that legal gun restrictions would stop mass shootings. The right believes that drug prohibition stops usage of illegal drugs. It should be obvious by now that drug prohibition does not stop usage of illegal drugs, just as gun control does not stop mass shootings. This is why individual freedom is so important. Every prohibition of the activities of innocent people backfires. The 'war on drugs' created tenfold more victims than the drugs themselves. The current 'gun grabbing' rhetoric, if put in place (leave the constitution out of this argument for the moment), would have the same result. Punishing the activity which creates a victim is the only way to address any of these issues.

If someone on drugs hurts another, the drugs are not the crime... hurting another person is the crime, and it is already illegal. If someone hurts another with a gun, the gun is not the crime... hurting another person is the crime, and it is already illegal. I understand the outcry to do something in the wake of horrific acts committed by people. Unfortunately, the answer that is always floated is more laws and more government tyranny over the individual... and those only serve to create more violence and less peace. In this insecure world, there is no way to have security through laws, because desperate people do desperate things. Laws are meaningless to a desperate person. Be knowledgeable of the dangers in this world and protect yourself accordingly. This may not give us all 'warm fuzzies', but it is the reality of the world we live in, and the only real answer.

40) I've been thinking quite a bit about what I believe is an emergency in this country. That emergency is rampant

obesity, and the complications that it creates. A major by-product of this obesity is an epidemic of early onset diabetes. The overall health of most people, and much more-so in low-income people declines year after year after year. It is common for people to attempt to identify one culprit for just about everything they see as a problem. Republicans blame Democrats. Democrats blame Republicans. Independents blame them both. But in this case, the problem is extremely complex.

There are many moving pieces of this puzzle. Big corporations have never had a conscience and never will. Big Food and Big Pharma have proven time and time again that profit is all that matters. They provide false information, formatted in such a way as to deceive the public. For these large corporations, every day that they can keep their gravy trains running is a good day. Millions of people look to government to protect the public from these corporations and the poison that they peddle. But this formula is flawed. Big government is the tool that facilitates the ability of the large corporations to penetrate markets, forcing public use of their products and growing their market share. Big corporations control big government. The bigger government becomes, the bigger the corporations become that control big government. In my opinion, the sugar industry is killing us all. Our foods are full of sugar in its various forms. Our drinks, even drinks that are perceived as healthy, such as fruit juice, are loaded with sugar.

The sugar industry bought and paid for scientists decades ago that convinced us all that it was fat... not sugar... that was the main cause of obesity and health problems. Today, many of us know that we were all duped, and it was government that was used as the lackey for the sugar industry who spread their message for them. Sugar triggers the release of insulin, a normal process... unless there is too much sugar. Too much sugar creates fat storage. When we eat ten times more sugar than our bodies need every day, you can imagine how much excess fat is created in our bodies. The sugar lobby prevented sugar from being included in nutritional guidelines (which include fat, calories, carbohydrates) as a percentage of recommended daily allowances from being printed on product labels. School lunches have been infiltrated by big food, and fresh foods have been replaced with pre-packaged or simple-to-prepare foods because they are cheaper and easier to use, and kids are already addicted to them.

Our society is addicted to sugar. Do you think that the sugar industry cares about how its market penetration will eventually bankrupt this country due to the cost of health care related to the diabetes epidemic? Of course not. Big tobacco knew early on that smoking cigarettes was a cause of lung cancer, but rather than take their products off the market, they just bought elected officials instead. Clearly, government is not the answer to this problem. Government shares responsibility for it by working as a shill for Big Food. Most people go back to the same place as always... more laws... more regulation. But what they fail to realize is that when government gets involved, they have instant credibility with the public. If the sugar lobby convinces government to include too much sugar in their dietary guidelines, that is a windfall for the sugar industry... and this is what happened.

The best diet is a diet with real food… not with excess sugar, salt, preservatives, and unidentifiable chemicals. But this diet requires effort. We all have busy lives, and just keeping up with our daily grind makes it more challenging to eat a diet than is healthier. A government which is owned and controlled by large corporations will never tell you this simple fact. Growing government will just end up with more growing waistlines. If government was really acting for the benefit of the people, it would not be bargaining with the corporations that produce toxic foods, and are making this country like a train about to crash into a mountain. If you want to solve this problem, get involved in your communities and let the people know that there is a better way. A large, central government which is controlled by financial interests will never do this.

41) Life cycle of a law: A) One person or a small number of people do something bad; B) Law is made in response; C) Much larger number of people are arrested, fined and possibly killed in the process. They say one bad apple doesn't spoil the barrel. This is not true in legislation. The typical response to one bad apple ruins far more lives than the original act, which results in the new legislation. Don't destroy the barrel full of good apples to punish the one that is already rotten.

42) I want to challenge your opinions on what is conventional. I highlight laws, because we were all taught that we should obey them. Looking at criminal law, tens of millions of people have been arrested or have lost their lives due to the invention of criminal status for peaceful activities

that are not in the interests of government. We have been taught that anyone who does not obey these laws is a criminal and must be punished. This is a slippery slope. Anything can be prohibited by law, and often times these laws creating prohibition are ended, and suddenly the activity which was so heinous that government took away your rights due to suspicion of violating that law... Later on, these activities became just fine, once government took a piece of the action. Alcohol, cannabis, even prostitution in Nevada were suddenly just fine once government was able to share the profits. This is an example of why laws which create criminals must have a victim. Otherwise, we are only servants at the whim of legislators or regulators. Prohibition violates the very foundation of a free country, controlled by the people.

43) Excess government will always happen, unless the people stand up to stop it. The new world was developed for individual freedom and opportunity. As government took hold in the East, people headed West for freedom and opportunity. As excess government took over in the West, people ran to the middle. Now, both coasts, dripping in excess government, are trying to take over the middle, hence the national popular vote efforts spreading around the country, and the continued growth of the federal government and the related removal of power from states and local jurisdictions, flying in the face of the 10th Amendment. Sorry, founding fathers. Most of us ignored you and excess government will take over the middle as well.

More government always means less freedom. Some of

us still see that, but those of us who see this trend and still want to fight for individual freedom are insulted by those who embrace the tyranny of government, instead describing this tyranny with flowery terms rather than the ugly, iron fist that it really is. Helpful hint: progressives are not patriots. The real patriots are the people who keep the purpose of this country in mind, do not rubber stamp the notion that our flag stands for freedom even if freedom disappears completely, and are not afraid to speak about the goal of individual freedom, front and center to the very end.

44) 33% of all adults in the United States have been arrested. 33%! The majority of these arrests are due to possession of an illegal substance. Possession, i.e., not hurting anyone. This has been used as a tool, since the Nixon administration against their perceived political enemies, as was admitted by Nixon aide John Ehrlichman. This created the war on drugs, which tore apart families, mostly in densely populated areas. Enforcement became rampant. Alongside this is the current situation that the USA now imprisons the highest percentage of its citizens of all countries in the entire world. More than Russia. More than China, more than North Korea... The entire world!

This is government run wild against its people. To make matters worse, with all these people arrested and/or imprisoned, while the costs are in the Trillions of Dollars, it has not reduced drug use at all. The existence of drug gangs is the expected response to the prohibition of drugs. This also increases the violence and gun death. In Portugal, mere possession of drugs is not illegal, and Portugal looks at illicit drug use as more of a health problem. This has reduced usage by an estimated 50%, reduced overdose deaths and drug related HIV infections by 90%, and all but ended drug violence in that country. If we were to do that here, families would not be torn apart at near the rate we have today. Drug use dropping is a good thing. If something that people want en masse is not illegal, there is no related organized crime. So, if we simply changed the legal classification of drugs from a crime to a medical problem, murders plummet, overdoses plummet, addiction plummets, HIV infections plummet, the cost of paying for all this enforcement and incarceration plummets, and gun deaths also plummet.

45) Every year, myriad people swear an oath to support and defend the constitution of the United States. Many of them are lying. The oath is meaningless to them. They do all they can to circumvent the constitution. I think that there should be a severe penalty for this. But sadly, even treason is never prosecuted against government officials at any level. Today, presidential candidates entice voters by offering creative ways to get around the constitution to give them what they claim to want. The presidential oath of office includes the promise to preserve, protect, and defend the constitution of the United States. I can't remember the last President to fulfill this promise.

There is no discipline in politics… and no punishment for lying… and the people cheer these criminals on because they share their precious initial next to their name. These are not victimless criminals. They make the American People victims of their actions every year, by the millions. Say what you want about the constitution. It was ineffective (true). It is old and you did not vote for it (true). But if I might add… if the politicians did not find ways to get around the constitution, the people of this country would be in far better shape than they are today, and individual freedom would be more of a reality. Today, with politicians doing all they can to get around the constitution, individual freedom has largely perished from this Earth.

46) Before you worship the omnipotent state and admire its purity and altruism, remember these (these were legal, and many were done by the state): A) Slavery; B) Women were denied the right to vote; C) Disabled and mentally ill people were forcibly sterilized by the state; D) Native American children were taken from reservations by the US government; E) Japanese Americans were imprisoned in internment camps in WWII; F) Spousal rape; and G) Segregation. Still illegal in some states: A) Possession of a plant; B) Certain sexual positions between consenting adults; C) Raw milk across state lines; D) Selling hot dogs without a permit; and E) Feeding homeless people. Laws are often immoral. Because something is legal does not make it good, just as when something is illegal it is not automatically bad.

47) When you take a side on an issue, unless you have personal experience with the subject, you assess credibility and that helps you lean toward your beliefs. Unless, of course, all you do is parrot whatever your 'team' says. After all, it's easier and takes less time if you just back your team… even though your team doesn't care about you one tiny bit (well, except for wanting your money and your

votes). Let's take this a step further. Each team brings in 'experts' to prove their case, and the other team does what they can do discredit the other team's experts. Those experts are almost always paid to say what each side wants them to say. It's just like a court trial, but this is the court of public opinion. Personally, people lose credibility in my mind when they stand to gain financially if they win in the court of public opinion, and the people use government to force the winning views on everyone else.

What bothers me is that people with no personal knowledge or experience with the issue du jour will take a side with such passion, that they are so positive that they are right that they attack people who see things differently... with vitriol... even though they cannot provide proof positive either way. Examples: climate change, vaccines, 9/11, political disagreements, mass shootings, religions, he said-she said, allegations of sexual misconduct, who killed who, police misconduct, any criminal accusations, etc. It never ceases to amaze me how people can be so positive of one side or the other that they will get violent against anyone who disagrees, even though they have no personal knowledge at all about the situation or event.

The truth of most disputed issues is typically somewhere in the middle. It is not unusual that there is correct information on both sides of an issue, but people want the absolute. The reality of disputed situations must be pretty boring, because it seems that no one wants that. This world is about fighting and winning at all cost. This is the reason why there will never be peace on Earth. But since we are here... I suggest that we make the best of things while we occupy this planet. True tolerance – not just the fake, liberal tolerance, which is really quite violent, but real tolerance of the actions of other people that do not hurt you, as well as the opinions of people who disagree… True tolerance is the key to the most peace there can be on Earth (well, that and the smallest amount of government possible).

48) Problem solving from a government's perspective. Problem: U.S. Citizens want to be free. Our power is limited due to that pesky constitution. A) Identify something important to the masses. Food, shelter and medical care are foundational and great examples. B) Make it prohibitively expensive, or hard to get. C) Control the production and distribution by making laws and regulations which drive up the price to impossible levels, and severely penalize people who try to provide these items to others without your consent. D) Let time pass and watch how desperate people get. Make sure the media keeps talking about this 'problem' you have created. E) Offer a solution that appears to solve the public's problems. Offer to provide these items with little or no direct cost to them. Make them afraid of what happens if they don't follow your directives. You can use the structure proposed by Karl Marx and implemented by Vladimir Lenin. People are more interested in cell phones than history. Just get an edgy and energetic person to deliver this message. The most desperate people will make this person a superstar. F) The public will embrace the plan out of desperation. If anyone resists, remember… fear is the best way to keep them from becoming a major hindrance. Problem solved. You have destroyed individual freedom in

a free country without an obvious battle.

49) It seems like a group of sore losers are on the cusp of killing the electoral college. These same people want to get rid of the 2nd Amendment. There are also those who would prefer that the freedom of speech provision in the 1st Amendment be changed to limit speech which offends people. A state-run news source has been suggested. The 4th Amendment was badly damaged with the Patriot Act and the subsequent NSA spying on US citizens. It continues to erode more and more each year. The 5th Amendment was ignored with eminent domain and civil asset forfeiture. The government hates jury trials, and in civil cases, they uniformly petition to reject the defense requests for a jury.

The 6th Amendment is still in place, however the system bullies defendants to accept plea bargains in order to avoid a higher cost of defense or the risk of even worse charges. This is one reason why so many innocent people are in prison. The 7th amendment is steamrolled by government regulators every day. The 8th amendment was crushed by civil asset forfeiture, and the common killings of suspects during the arrest process. The 10th Amendment has to be targeted for destruction by the new goals of central planning at the national level, and federal regulatory arms growing in size and scope.

The 3rd seems relatively intact, and the 9th has had some challenges, but nothing that notable. It is the bill of rights that makes our flag stand for freedom. Every time government tramples another of these first ten amendments, the light of freedom is diminished. But sure… keep putting your political party's desires over the foundation of the country. If the electoral college is lost, there will never be a choice other than Democrats or Republicans for President, until the people who actively destroy the work of the architects of this country succeed in entirety, and the country self-destructs. This can still be avoided, but it's now a long shot. Of course, the government wants to get rid of the bill of rights because it limits their power. When the people also have this goal... we are done.

50) The bill of rights was the glue that held this country together. It wasn't perfect, but it held off the anti-freedom people from total destruction of the country for over two hundred and forty years, when the process would have taken about fifty to one hundred years without the bill of rights. Now there are people that want to take away your natural right to defend yourself. These same people want to completely impede innovation, which was most successful by private citizens. These same people want to take the lion's share of your earnings and provide your basic necessities without regard to your preferences. These same people want to control your speech, because they are easily offended unless you talk the way they want you to talk. These same people want five counties in the country to pick the president over all fifty states. These same people loudly shout the same anti-capitalist message that was written by Vladimir Lenin in 1897. These same people would happily rescind the bill of rights, because it is inconvenient for them, and they 'never had the opportunity to vote for it'.

All the while, as freedoms are stripped from the people, schools will teach that our flag stands for freedom. Our generation were stewards of the USA, and we had one simple job: to sustain the structure and vision of the nation's founders. We have done a terrible job of this. As George Carlin mused, "It's a great big, red, white and blue stroke job." We are embroiled in a fight to maintain the very foundation of this country… if we fail, be sure to turn the lights off once all freedom has left the building as we are the next USSR, but with flowers and unicorns… until the mass killing ramps up again, as it always has in centrally-controlled totalitarian societies.

End

CPSIA information can be obtained
at www.ICGtesting.com
Printed in the USA
LVHW031917160922
728572LV00003B/89